Heart Healthy Cookbook

Publications International, Ltd.

Favorite Brand Name Recipes at www.fbnr.com

Pictured on the front cover *(clockwise from top left):* Asian Beef Wraps *(page 48),* Blueberry Bread Pudding with Caramel Sauce *(page 90),* Tangy Italian Chicken Sandwich *(page 58)* and Sicilian-Style Pasta Salad *(page 26).*

Pictured on the back cover *(clockwise from top):* Speedy Spaghetti with Sausage *(page 54),* Brownie Cake Delight *(page 76)* and Grilled Honey Garlic Pork Chop *(page 42).*

ISBN: 0-7853-6124-3

Manufactured in China.

8 7 6 5 4 3 2 1

Nutritional Analysis: The nutritional information that appears with each recipe was submitted in part by the participating companies and associations. Every effort has been made to check the accuracy of these numbers. However, because numerous variables account for a wide range of values for certain foods, nutritive analyses in this book should be considered approximate.

Microwave Cooking: Microwave ovens vary in wattage. Use the cooking times as guidelines and check for doneness before adding more time.

Preparation/Cooking Times: Preparation times are based on the approximate amount of time required to assemble the recipe before cooking, baking, chilling or serving. These times include preparation steps such as measuring, chopping and mixing. The fact that some preparations and cooking can be done simultaneously is taken into account. Preparation of optional ingredients and serving suggestions is not included.

Eating Right

Getting Started

By choosing this publication, you must be ready to adopt a new way of eating. Congratulations! That decision will mean a healthier you, and we will help you get there. By preparing heart-healthy meals, you'll not only feel better and more energized, you'll also lower your risk of health problems such as heart disease, diabetes and certain cancers. And the best part is, the foods you'll be eating are delicious and filling.

In a search for the "perfect" diet, there are many choices. The most successful ones are not diets at all, but are actually new ways of eating that become part of your normal lifestyle. Don't be fooled by diet schemes that make unrealistic demands such as drinking a liquid diet, focusing on one food group, fasting or starving yourself, or requiring unbalanced meal plans. The best plan for heart-healthy living is to gradually change the foods you eat. The recipes found here are not gimmicks—they're made with foods chockful of satisfying complex carbohydrates, brimming with fiber to give you a feeling of fullness, and rich in nutrients to keep you naturally healthy.

Compared to the standard American diet, the eating plan you are about to embark upon is likely much healthier. You're encouraged to eat a variety of complex carbohydrates such as fruits, vegetables, legumes and whole grains, along with some dairy and protein foods, to keep your body in tip-top shape. One note of caution: People with diabetes need to carefully watch the amount of carbohydrates in their diet, so some of these recipes may not fit into their meal plans.

Carbohydrate Consciousness

Many recent diet trends have given carbohydrates an undeserved bad name. Complex carbohydrates help to jump-start your metabolism. They are relatively low in calories and are often naturally rich in fiber, which is especially helpful if you are trying to lose weight. (Fiber helps you feel full, so you are less likely to overeat.) Carbohydrates and protein each contain only four calories per gram, whereas fat contains nine calories per gram.

Another reason eating carbohydrates is encouraged is because the body processes them differently from fat. Fat is broken down, absorbed and stored by the body without much effort, while carbohydrates and protein are more difficult for the body to break down, absorb, process, store and use. Because of this, your body uses more calories to break down carbohydrates and protein. This means there are likely fewer calories left over to get stored as fat.

The Fuss Over Fiber

Fiber *is* a big deal—it's recommended that all healthy people eat 20 to 35 grams of fiber each day. Increasing the amount of soluble fiber in your diet has been shown to lower blood cholesterol, which is important since high blood cholesterol is a major risk factor for heart disease. Both soluble and insoluble fibers slow the rate at which your stomach empties. They also enable the sugars in your meal to be absorbed slowly, so you'll feel full a little longer.

As you change your eating habits and gradually add more fiber-rich complex carbohydrates to your diet, it's absolutely essential that you also drink more water. Without enough fluids, the extra fiber will likely backfire on you and make you gassy and constipated.

The Skinny on Fat and Cholesterol

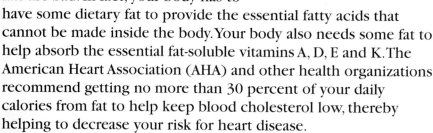

Besides filling up on fiber and complex carbohydrates, it's important to make low-fat choices. Keep in mind that you do need some fat each day, and not all fats are bad. In fact, your body has to have some dietary fat to provide the essential fatty acids that cannot be made inside the body. Your body also needs some fat to help absorb the essential fat-soluble vitamins A, D, E and K. The American Heart Association (AHA) and other health organizations recommend getting no more than 30 percent of your daily calories from fat to help keep blood cholesterol low, thereby helping to decrease your risk for heart disease.

The foods we eat contain three kinds of fat. Try to stick to monounsaturated fats, which are predominant in olive and canola oils. Saturated fats, found in animal foods such as meat and dairy products, as well as certain vegetable oils such as coconut and palm kernel oils, should be avoided as much as possible—they should make up no more than a third of the total fats you eat. Other types of fats, such as polyunsaturated (found in most vegetable oils) and hydrogenated (found in most processed and packaged products), should also be used sparingly.

Eating too much saturated fat and cholesterol has been found to increase the level of cholesterol in your body, which may contribute to the development of heart disease. Dietary cholesterol comes only from animal products (mainly meat, eggs and dairy), so it's wise to limit your intake of these foods. While it's important to watch the amount of cholesterol you eat, it has been found that reducing the amount of fat (especially saturated fat) in your diet will help reduce your risk of heart disease more than just decreasing the amount of cholesterol alone. However, most foods high in saturated fat are also high in cholesterol, so cutting down your saturated fat intake will probably lower your cholesterol intake as well. And the good news is that studies have shown even small reductions in one's cholesterol level can significantly reduce the risk of heart disease.

Salty Issues

With so much emphasis placed on fat and cholesterol, it's easy to forget about sodium in your diet. For heart-healthy living, it's generally advised to keep your salt intake at low to moderate levels. The American Heart Association recommends no more than 2,400 milligrams of sodium per day, which is slightly over a teaspoon of table salt. (Most Americans consume over twice that much.) A diet high in sodium may contribute to high blood pressure in some people, and high blood pressure is another big risk factor for heart disease and stroke. Simply purchasing reduced-sodium products at the supermarket can make a significant difference in the amount of sodium you consume each day. And, of course, taste all prepared foods before adding additional salt—they might not need any!

Activity: The Final Ingredient

You've heard it before. You know it's true. It's extremely important to do some physical activity on a regular basis. Studies have shown that inactive people have twice the risk of developing heart disease as those who lead active lifestyles. You don't need a complex workout—the activity can be as simple as walking, and it doesn't have to be done in one continuous session. But physical activity shouldn't be ignored or overlooked, as it is a crucial part of heart-healthy living.

Get Going!

Depending on your current habits, heart-healthy living may require an overhaul of your lifestyle. The recipes in this publication are a good place to start. They are all low in fat and cholesterol, of course, but they're more than that—they're also high in fiber and rich in nutrients, as you can see in the nutritional analyses of the recipes. You can't go wrong if you eat a wide variety of the choices presented and if you do so in moderation. Eat smart, stay active and enjoy!

Appetizers & Snacks

Spicy Vegetable Quesadillas

1 small zucchini, chopped
½ cup chopped green bell
   pepper
½ cup chopped onion
2 cloves garlic, minced
½ teaspoon chili powder
½ teaspoon ground cumin

8 (6-inch) flour tortillas
1 cup (4 ounces) shredded
   reduced-fat Cheddar
   cheese
¼ cup chopped fresh
   cilantro

1. Spray large nonstick skillet with cooking spray. Heat over medium heat until hot. Add vegetables, garlic, chili powder and cumin; cook and stir 3 to 4 minutes or until vegetables are crisp-tender. Remove vegetables; wipe skillet clean.

2. Spoon vegetable mixture evenly over half of each tortilla. Sprinkle with cheese and cilantro. Fold each tortilla in half.

3. Spray same skillet with cooking spray. Add tortillas and heat 1 to 2 minutes per side over medium heat or until lightly browned. Cut into thirds before serving.   *Makes 8 servings*

Nutrients per Serving: Calories: 153, Calories from Fat: 22%, Total Fat: 4 g, Saturated Fat: 1 g, Protein: 7 g, Carbohydrate: 23 g, Cholesterol: 8 mg, Sodium: 201 mg, Fiber: 1 g, Iron: <1 mg, Calcium: 112 mg, Vitamin A: 56 RE, Vitamin C: 15 mg, Sugar: 1 g
Dietary Exchanges: 1½ Starch, 1 Meat

Spicy Vegetable Quesadillas

Buffalo Chicken Tenders

3 tablespoons Louisiana-style hot sauce
½ teaspoon paprika
¼ teaspoon ground red pepper
1 pound chicken tenders
½ cup fat-free blue cheese dressing
¼ cup reduced-fat sour cream
2 tablespoons crumbled blue cheese
1 medium red bell pepper, cut into ½-inch slices

1. Preheat oven to 375°F. Combine hot sauce, paprika and ground red pepper in small bowl; brush on all surfaces of chicken. Place chicken in greased 11×7-inch baking pan. Cover; marinate in refrigerator 30 minutes.

2. Bake, uncovered, about 15 minutes or until chicken is no longer pink in center.

3. Combine blue cheese dressing, sour cream and blue cheese in small serving bowl. Garnish as desired. Serve with chicken and bell pepper.   *Makes 10 servings*

Nutrients per Serving: Calories: 83, Calories from Fat: 27%, Total Fat: 2 g, Saturated Fat: 1 g, Protein: 9 g, Carbohydrate: 5 g, Cholesterol: 27 mg, Sodium: 180 mg, Fiber: 0 g, Iron: <1 mg, Calcium: 14 mg, Vitamin A: 19 RE, Vitamin C: 7 mg
Dietary Exchanges: ½ Starch, 1 Meat

Chicken tenders are the lean, tender strips that are found on the underside of the breast. They are skinless and boneless and have virtually no waste.

Buffalo Chicken Tenders

Greek Spinach-Cheese Rolls

1 loaf (1 pound) frozen
    bread dough
1 package (10 ounces)
    frozen chopped
    spinach, thawed and
    squeezed dry
¾ cup (3 ounces) crumbled
    feta cheese

½ cup (2 ounces) shredded
    reduced-fat Monterey
    Jack cheese
4 green onions, thinly
    sliced
1 teaspoon dried dill weed
½ teaspoon garlic powder
½ teaspoon black pepper

1. Thaw bread dough according to package directions. Spray 15 muffin cups with nonstick cooking spray; set aside. Roll out dough on lightly floured surface to 15×9-inch rectangle. (If dough is springy and difficult to roll, cover with plastic wrap and let rest 5 minutes to relax.) Position dough so long edge runs parallel to edge of work surface.

2. Combine spinach, cheeses, green onions, dill weed, garlic powder and pepper in large bowl; mix well.

3. Sprinkle spinach mixture evenly over dough to within 1 inch of long edges. Starting at long edge, roll up snugly, pinching seam closed. Place seam side down; cut roll with serrated knife into 1-inch-wide slices. Place slices, cut sides up, in prepared muffin cups. Cover with plastic wrap; let stand 30 minutes in warm place until rolls are slightly puffy.

4. Preheat oven to 375°F. Bake 20 to 25 minutes or until golden. Serve warm or at room temperature. Rolls can be stored in refrigerator in airtight container up to 2 days.

Makes 15 servings (1 roll each)

Nutrients per Serving: Calories: 111, Calories from Fat: 24%, Total Fat: 3 g, Saturated Fat: 2 g, Protein: 5 g, Carbohydrate: 16 g, Cholesterol: 8 mg, Sodium: 267 mg, Fiber: <1 g, Sugar: <1 g
Dietary Exchanges: 1 Starch, ½ Meat, ½ Fat

Greek Spinach-Cheese Rolls

Chicken Nachos

22 (about 1 ounce)
GUILTLESS GOURMET®
Baked Tortilla Chips
(yellow, red or blue
corn)

½ cup (4 ounces) cooked
and shredded boneless
chicken breast

¼ cup chopped green
onions

¼ cup (1 ounce) grated
Cheddar cheese

Sliced green and red
chilies (optional)

Microwave Directions:
Spread tortilla chips on flat microwave-safe plate. Sprinkle
chicken, onions and cheese over chips. Microwave on HIGH
30 seconds until cheese starts to bubble. Serve hot. Garnish with
chilies, if desired.   *Makes 22 nachos*

Conventional Directions: Preheat oven to 325°F. Spread tortilla
chips on baking sheet. Sprinkle chicken, onions and cheese over
chips. Bake about 5 minutes or until cheese starts to bubble.
Serve hot.

Nutrients per Serving (1 nacho): Calories: 13, Calories from Fat: 12%,
Total Fat: <1 g, Saturated Fat: 0 g, Protein: 1 g, Carbohydrate: 2 g,
Cholesterol: 3 mg, Sodium: 24 mg, Fiber: 0 g

When a recipe calls for
chopped cooked chicken, it can be difficult to
judge how much chicken to purchase. As a
guideline, one whole chicken breast (about
10 ounces) will yield about 1 cup of chopped
cooked chicken.

Savory Sweet Potato Sticks

Prep Time: 25 minutes   **Bake Time:** 15 minutes

3 medium sweet potatoes
    (about 1½ pounds)
3 cups KELLOGG'S® RICE
    KRISPIES® cereal,
    crushed to ¾ cup
½ teaspoon garlic salt
¼ teaspoon onion salt

⅛ teaspoon cayenne
½ cup all-purpose flour
2 egg whites
2 tablespoons water
    Vegetable cooking spray
    Salsa (optional)

1. Wash potatoes and cut lengthwise into ½-inch slices. Cut slices into ½-inch strips. Set aside.

2. In shallow pan or plate, combine Kellogg's Rice Krispies® cereal and spices. Set aside. Place flour in second shallow pan or plate. Set aside. Beat together egg whites and water. Set aside. Coat potatoes with flour, shaking off excess. Dip coated potatoes in egg mixture, then coat with cereal mixture. Place in single layer on foil-lined baking sheet coated with cooking spray.

3. Bake at 400°F about 30 minutes or until lightly browned. Serve hot with salsa, if desired.   *Makes 15 servings*

Nutrients per Serving: Calories: 82, Calories from Fat: 1%, Total Fat: <1 g, Saturated Fat: <1 g, Protein: 2 g, Carbohydrate: 18 g, Cholesterol: 0 mg, Sodium: 111 mg, Fiber: 2 g, Iron: 1 mg, Calcium: 14 mg, Vitamin A: 1014 RE, Vitamin C: 14 mg, Sugar: 6 g
Dietary Exchanges: 1 Starch

Reuben Bites

24 party rye bread slices
½ cup prepared fat-free
    Thousand Island
    dressing
6 ounces turkey pastrami,
    very thinly sliced

1 cup (4 ounces) shredded
    reduced-fat Swiss
    cheese
1 cup alfalfa sprouts

1. Preheat oven to 400°F.

2. Arrange bread slices on nonstick baking sheet. Bake 5 minutes or until lightly toasted.

3. Spread 1 teaspoon dressing onto each bread slice; top with pastrami, folding slices to fit bread slices. Sprinkle evenly with cheese.

4. Bake 5 minutes or until hot. Top evenly with sprouts. Transfer to serving plate; garnish, if desired. *Makes 12 servings*

Nutrients per Serving: Calories: 142, Calories from Fat: 21%, Total Fat: 3 g, Saturated Fat: 1 g, Protein: 9 g, Carbohydrate: 19 g, Cholesterol: 15 mg, Sodium: 516 mg, Fiber: <1 g, Iron: 1 mg, Calcium: 143 mg, Vitamin A: 21 RE, Vitamin C: <1 mg
Dietary Exchanges: 1 Starch, 1 Meat

Alfalfa sprouts are available in the produce sections of most large supermarkets. Store them in the refrigerator, in the ventilated plastic container in which they were sold, for no more than 2 or 3 days.

Roasted Garlic & Spinach Spirals

1 whole head fresh garlic
3 cups fresh spinach leaves
1 can (15 ounces) white
    beans, rinsed and
    drained
1 teaspoon dried oregano
    leaves

¼ teaspoon black pepper
⅛ teaspoon ground red
    pepper
7 (7-inch) flour tortillas

1. Preheat oven to 400°F. Trim top of garlic just enough to cut tips off center cloves; discard tips. Moisten head of garlic with water; wrap in foil. Bake 45 minutes or until garlic is soft and has a mellow garlicky aroma; cool. Remove garlic from skin by squeezing between fingers and thumb; place in food processor.

2. Rinse spinach leaves; pat dry with paper towels. Remove stems; discard. Finely shred leaves by stacking and cutting several leaves at a time. Place in medium bowl.

3. Add beans, oregano, black pepper and red pepper to food processor; process until smooth. Add to spinach; mix well. Spread mixture evenly onto tortillas; roll up. Trim ½ inch off ends of rolls; discard. Cut rolls into 1-inch pieces. Transfer to serving plates; garnish, if desired. *Makes 10 servings*

Tip: For best results, cover tortilla rolls and refrigerate 1 to 2 hours before slicing.

Nutrients per Serving (4 pieces): Calories: 139, Calories from Fat: 13%, Total Fat: 2 g, Saturated Fat: <1 g, Protein: 6 g, Carbohydrate: 25 g, Cholesterol: 0 mg, Sodium: 293 mg, Fiber: 1 g, Iron: 3 mg, Calcium: 88 mg, Vitamin A: 115 RE, Vitamin C: 6 mg, Sugar: <1 g
Dietary Exchanges: 1 vegetable, 1½ Starch

Roasted Garlic & Spinach Spirals

Caponata Spread

1½ tablespoons olive or
    vegetable oil
1 medium eggplant, diced
    (about 4 cups)
1 medium onion, chopped
1½ cups water
1 envelope LIPTON® RECIPE
    SECRETS® Savory Herb
    with Garlic Soup Mix

2 tablespoons chopped
    fresh parsley (optional)
Salt and ground black
    pepper to taste
Pita chips or thinly sliced
    Italian or French bread

In 10-inch nonstick skillet, heat oil over medium heat and cook eggplant with onion 3 minutes. Add ½ cup water. Reduce heat to low and simmer covered 3 minutes. Stir in Savory Herb with Garlic Soup mix blended with remaining 1 cup water. Bring to a boil over high heat. Reduce heat to low and simmer uncovered, stirring occasionally, 20 minutes. Stir in parsley, salt and pepper. Serve with pita chips.   *Makes about 4 cups spread*

Nutrients per Serving (2 tablespoons): Calories: 13, Calories from Fat: 43%, Total Fat: 1 g, Saturated Fat: <1 g, Protein: <1 g, Carbohydrate: 2 g, Cholesterol: 0 mg, Sodium: 60 mg, Fiber: <1 g, Iron: <1 mg, Calcium: 2 mg, Vitamin A: 1 RE, Vitamin C: <1 mg, Sugar: 1 g
Dietary Exchanges: Free

When purchasing eggplant,
look for a firm eggplant that is heavy for its size,
with tight, glossy, deeply-colored skin and a bright
green stem.

Potato Pancake Appetizers

3 medium Colorado russet
    potatoes, peeled and
    grated
1 egg
2 tablespoons all-purpose
    flour
1 teaspoon salt
¼ teaspoon black pepper
1½ cups grated zucchini
    (2 small)
1 cup grated carrot
    (1 large)
1½ cup low-fat sour cream
    or plain yogurt
2 tablespoons finely
    chopped fresh basil
1 tablespoon chopped
    chives *or* 1½ teaspoons
    chili powder

Preheat oven to 425°F. Wrap potatoes in several layers of paper towels; squeeze to remove excess moisture. Beat egg, flour, salt and pepper in large bowl. Add potatoes, zucchini and carrot. mix well. Oil 2 nonstick baking sheets. Place vegetable mixture by heaping spoonfuls onto baking sheets; flatten slightly. Bake 8 to 15 minutes until bottoms are browned. Turn; bake 5 to 10 minutes more. Stir together sour cream and herbs; serve with warm pancakes. *Makes about 24 appetizer pancakes*

Favorite recipe from **Colorado Potato Administrative Committee**

Nutrients per Serving (1 pancake): Calories: 30, Calories from Fat: 19%, Total Fat: 1 g, Saturated Fat: <1 g, Protein: 1 g, Carbohydrate: 5 g, Cholesterol: 11 mg, Sodium: 106 mg, Fiber: 1 g, Iron: <1 mg, Calcium: 12 mg, Vitamin A: 144 RE, Vitamin C: 3 mg, Sugar: 1 g
Dietary Exchanges: ½ Starch

Portobello Mushrooms Sesame

4 large portobello
  mushrooms
2 tablespoons sweet rice
  wine

2 tablespoons reduced-
  sodium soy sauce
2 cloves garlic, minced
1 teaspoon dark sesame oil

1. Remove and discard stems from mushrooms; set caps aside. Combine remaining ingredients in small bowl.

2. Brush both sides of mushrooms with soy sauce mixture. Grill mushrooms, top sides up, on covered grill over medium coals 3 to 4 minutes. Brush tops with soy sauce mixture and turn over; grill 2 minutes more or until mushrooms are lightly browned. Turn again and grill, basting frequently, 4 to 5 minutes or until tender when pressed with back of spatula. Remove mushrooms and cut diagonally into ½-inch-thick slices. *Makes 4 servings*

Nutrients per Serving: Calories: 67, Calories from Fat: 21%, Total Fat: 2 g, Saturated Fat: <1 g, Protein: 4 g, Carbohydrate: 9 g, Cholesterol: 0 mg, Sodium: 268 mg, Fiber: <1 g, Iron: 3 mg, Calcium: 13 mg, Vitamin A: 0 RE, Vitamin C: 6 mg
Dietary Exchanges: 2 Vegetable, ½ Fat

Rice wine is a sweet, golden wine made from fermented rice, often used to add sweetness and flavor to a variety of Asian dishes. Two Japanese rice wines are mirin and sake; mirin is often found in the gourmet or ethnic section of large supermarkets.

Portobello Mushrooms Sesame

Soups & Salads

Sicilian-Style Pasta Salad

1 pound dry rotini pasta
2 cans (14.5 ounces)
   CONTADINA® Recipe
   Ready Diced Tomatoes
   with Italian Herbs,
   undrained
1 cup sliced yellow bell
   pepper

1 cup sliced zucchini
8 ounces cooked bay
   shrimp
1 can (2.25 ounces) sliced
   pitted ripe olives,
   drained
2 tablespoons balsamic
   vinegar

1. Cook pasta according to package directions; drain.

2. Combine pasta, undrained tomatoes, bell pepper, zucchini, shrimp, olives and vinegar in large bowl; toss well.

3. Cover. Chill before serving.   *Makes 10 servings*

Nutrients per Serving: Calories: 111, Calories from Fat: 8%, Total Fat: 1 g, Saturated Fat: <1 g, Protein: 6 g, Carbohydrate: 19 g, Cholesterol: 0 mg, Sodium: 573 mg, Fiber: 2 g, Iron: <1 mg, Calcium: 39 mg, Vitamin A: 42 RE, Vitamin C: 47 mg, Sugar: 6 g
Dietary Exchanges: 1 Vegetable, 1 Starch, ½ Meat

Sicilian-Style Pasta Salad

Turkey Tortilla Soup

Preparation Time: 25 minutes

1 package (1¼ pounds)
  BUTTERBALL® Lean
  Fresh Ground Turkey
1 teaspoon olive oil
2 cans (14½ ounces each)
  100% fat free reduced
  sodium chicken broth
1 jar (16 ounces) mild or
  medium-hot salsa
1 can (11 ounces) Mexican-
  style corn, drained

1 tablespoon fresh lime
  juice
2 to 3 tablespoons
  chopped fresh cilantro
Salt and black pepper
2 ounces baked tortilla
  chips
Lime wedges

Heat oil in large saucepan over medium heat until hot. Brown
turkey in saucepan 6 to 8 minutes or until no longer pink, stirring
to separate meat. Add chicken broth, salsa, corn and lime juice to
saucepan. Reduce heat to low; simmer, covered, about 10 minutes.
Ladle into bowls. Sprinkle with cilantro. Add salt and pepper to
taste. Serve with tortilla chips and wedge of lime.

Makes 8 servings

Note: To make your own tortilla strips, cut flour tortillas into thin
strips and bake in 400°F oven until crisp. Serve on top of soup.

Nutrients per Serving: Calories: 218, Calories from Fat: 33%, Total Fat: 8 g,
Saturated Fat: 2 g, Protein: 19 g, Carbohydrate: 16 g, Cholesterol: 53 mg,
Sodium: 820 mg, Fiber: 2 g, Iron: 3 mg, Calcium: 34 mg, Vitamin A: 5 RE,
Vitamin C: 6 mg, Sugar: 4 g
Dietary Exchanges: 1 Starch, 2 Meat, ½ Fat

Black Bean and Rice Salad

2 cups cooked rice, cooled to room temperature
1 cup cooked black beans*
1 medium tomato, seeded and chopped
½ cup (2 ounces) shredded Cheddar cheese (optional)
1 tablespoon snipped parsley
¼ cup prepared light Italian dressing
1 tablespoon lime juice
Lettuce leaves

*Substitute canned black beans, drained, for the cooked beans, if desired.

Combine rice, beans, tomato, cheese, and parsley in large bowl. Pour dressing and lime juice over rice mixture; toss lightly. Serve on lettuce leaves. *Makes 4 servings*

Favorite recipe from **USA Rice Federation**

Nutrients per Serving: Calories: 210, Calories from Fat: 4%, Total Fat: 1 g, Protein: 7 g, Carbohydrate: 43 g, Cholesterol: 0 mg, Sodium: 560 mg, Fiber: 3 g

Skinny Waldorf Salad

2 cups chopped cored Red Delicious apples
1 cup chopped celery
1 cup cubed cooked boneless skinless chicken breast
¼ cup chopped green onions
3 tablespoons lemon nonfat yogurt
2 teaspoons fat-free mayonnaise
1 teaspoon toasted poppy seeds
¼ teaspoon salt
Dash pepper

Combine apples, celery, chicken and green onions in large bowl; set aside. For dressing, combine yogurt, mayonnaise, poppy seeds, salt and pepper in small bowl. Pour over apple mixture; toss to coat. Refrigerate, covered, at least 1 hour to allow flavors to blend. *Makes 4 servings*

Nutrients per Serving: Calories: 95, Calories from Fat: 13%, Total Fat: 1 g, Saturated Fat: <1 g, Protein: 9 g, Carbohydrate: 12 g, Cholesterol: 22 mg, Sodium: 205 mg, Fiber: 2 g, Calcium: 51 mg, Vitamin C: 6 mg, Sugar: 7 g
Dietary Exchanges: ½ vegetable, ½ Fruit, 1 Meat

Fajita Salad

1 beef sirloin steak
  (6 ounces)
¼ cup fresh lime juice
2 tablespoons chopped
  fresh cilantro
1 clove garlic, minced
1 teaspoon chili powder
2 red bell peppers
1 medium onion

1 teaspoon olive oil
1 cup garbanzo beans,
  rinsed and drained
4 cups mixed salad greens
1 tomato, cut into wedges
1 cup salsa
  Sour Cream (optional)
  Cilantro (optional)

1. Cut beef into 2×1×¼-inch strips. Place in resealable plastic food storage bag. Combine lime juice, cilantro, garlic and chili powder in small bowl. Pour over beef; seal bag. Let stand for 10 minutes, turning once.

2. Cut bell peppers into strips. Cut onion into slices. Heat olive oil in large nonstick skillet over medium-high heat until hot. Add bell peppers and onion. Cook and stir 6 minutes or until vegetables are crisp-tender. Remove from skillet. Add beef and marinade to skillet. Cook and stir 3 minutes or until meat is cooked through. Remove from heat. Add bell peppers, onion and garbanzo beans to skillet; toss to coat with pan juices. Cool slightly.

3. Divide salad greens evenly among serving plates. Top with beef mixture and tomato wedges. Serve with salsa. Garnish with sour cream and sprigs of cilantro, if desired.   *Makes 4 servings*

Nutrients per Serving: Calories: 181, Calories from Fat: 18%, Total Fat: 4 g, Saturated Fat: 1 g, Protein: 16 g, Carbohydrate: 25 g, Cholesterol: 22 mg, Sodium: 698 mg, Fiber: 6 g, Iron: 4 mg, Calcium: 83 mg, Vitamin A: 259 RE, Vitamin C: 81 mg, Sugar: 7 g
Dietary Exchanges: 1½ Starch, 1½ Meat

Fajita Salad

Butternut Bisque

1 teaspoon margarine or butter

1 large onion, coarsely chopped

1 medium butternut squash (about 1½ pounds), peeled, seeded and cut into ½-inch pieces

2 cans (about 14 ounces each) reduced-sodium or regular chicken broth, divided

½ teaspoon ground nutmeg or freshly grated nutmeg

⅛ teaspoon white pepper Plain nonfat yogurt and chives for garnish (optional)

Melt margarine in large saucepan over medium heat. Add onion; cook and stir 3 minutes.

Add squash and 1 can chicken broth; bring to a boil over high heat. Reduce heat to low; cover and simmer 20 minutes or until squash is very tender.

Process squash mixture, in 2 batches, in food processor until smooth. Return soup to saucepan; add remaining can of broth, nutmeg and pepper. Simmer, uncovered, 5 minutes, stirring occasionally.*

Ladle soup into soup bowls. Place yogurt in pastry bag fitted with round decorating tip. Pipe onto soup in decorative design. Garnish with chives, if desired.   *Makes about 5 cups (6 servings)*

*At this point, soup may be covered and refrigerated up to 2 days before serving. Reheat over medium heat, stirring occasionally.

Nutrients per Serving: Calories: 79, Calories from Fat: 9%, Total Fat: 1 g, Saturated Fat: <1 g, Protein: 5 g, Carbohydrate: 14 g, Cholesterol: 0 mg, Sodium: 107 mg, Fiber: 4 g, Iron: 2 mg, Calcium: 64 mg, Vitamin A: 800 RE, Vitamin C: 20 mg, Sugar: 5 g
Dietary Exchanges: 1 Starch

Butternut Bisque

Cool-as-a-Cucumber Salad

4 cups cooked UNCLE
   BEN'S® CONVERTED®
   Brand Original Rice
1 cup finely chopped
   seeded cucumber
¾ cup plain yogurt or sour
   cream
2 tablespoons finely
   chopped onion

1 tablespoon balsamic
   vinegar
2 teaspoons dried dill
   weed
1 teaspoon salt
¼ teaspoon black pepper

1. Rinse hot cooked rice under cold running water to cool; drain.

2. In large bowl, combine rice with remaining ingredients; mix well. Cover and refrigerate until well chilled to allow flavors to blend, about 4 hours.   *Makes 6 servings*

Nutrients per Serving: Calories: 162, Calories from Fat: 4%, Total Fat: 1 g, Saturated Fat: <1 g, Protein: 5 g, Carbohydrate: 33 g, Cholesterol: 2 mg, Sodium: 410 mg, Fiber: 1 g, Iron: 1 mg, Calcium: 67 mg, Vitamin A: 11 RE, Vitamin C: 2 mg, Sugar: 3 g
Dietary Exchanges: 2 Starch

Converted, or parboiled, rice is the unhulled grain that is soaked, processed by steam pressure and dried before milling. The result is a rice kernel that is more nutritious and less starchy than polished white rice. It takes longer to cook than white rice and absorbs more liquid during cooking.

Cool-as-a-Cucumber Salad

Calico Minestrone Soup

Prep Time: 5 minutes   **Cook Time:** 25 minutes

2 cans (14 ounces each)
   chicken broth
¼ cup uncooked small shell
   pasta
1 can (14½ ounces) DEL
   MONTE® Italian Recipe
   Stewed Tomatoes
1 can (8¾ ounces) *or* 1 cup
   kidney beans, drained

½ cup chopped cooked
   chicken or beef
1 carrot, cubed
1 stalk celery, sliced
½ teaspoon dried basil,
   crushed

1. Bring broth to boil in large saucepan; stir in pasta and boil
5 minutes.

2. Add remaining ingredients.

3. Reduce heat; cover and simmer 20 minutes. Garnish with
grated Parmesan cheese, if desired.

Makes approximately 6 servings (1 cup each)

Nutrients per Serving: Calories: 122, Calories from Fat: 22%, Total Fat: 3 g,
Saturated Fat: 1 g, Protein: 8 g, Carbohydrate: 16 g, Cholesterol: 10 mg,
Sodium: 844 mg, Fiber: 3 g, Iron: 1 mg, Calcium: 41 mg, Vitamin A: 373 RE,
Vitamin C: 3 mg, Sugar: 4 g
Dietary Exchanges: 1 Starch, ½ Meat, ½ Fat

Four-Season Fruit Slaw

Prep Time: 15 minutes   **Cook Time:** 5 minutes
Chill Time: 30 minutes

4 cups (10 ounces) DOLE® Classic Cole Slaw
½ cup DOLE® Chopped Dates or Pitted Prunes, chopped
⅓ cup DOLE® Golden or Seedless Raisins

¼ cup sliced green onions
½ cup fat free or reduced fat mayonnaise
2 tablespoons apricot or peach fruit spread
⅓ cup DOLE® Slivered Almonds, toasted

• Toss together cole slaw, dates, raisins and green onions in large serving bowl.

• Stir together mayonnaise and fruit spread until blended in small bowl. Add to cole slaw; toss well to evenly coat. Chill 30 minutes. Stir in almonds before serving.   *Makes 6 servings*

Nutrients per Serving: Calories: 143, Calories from Fat: 19%, Total Fat: 3 g, Saturated Fat: <1 g, Protein: 3 g, Carbohydrate: 28 g, Cholesterol: 0 mg, Sodium: 150 mg, Fiber: 3 g, Iron: 1 mg, Calcium: 33 mg, Vitamin A: 8 RE, Vitamin C: 16 mg, Sugar: 21 g
Dietary Exchanges: 1½ vegetable, 1½ Fruit, ½ Fat

Tangy Vegetable Salad

2 cups small broccoli florets
1 cup finely shredded red cabbage
¾ cup diced red bell pepper
1 medium carrot, shredded (about ½ cup)

½ cup bottled fat-free or reduced-fat ranch salad dressing
2 teaspoons prepared horseradish

Combine vegetables in large bowl. Combine salad dressing and horseradish. Pour over salad; toss to coat. Cover and refrigerate until ready to serve.   *Makes 3 cups*

Nutrients per Serving (½ cup): Calories: 56, Calories from Fat: 8%, Total Fat: 1 g, Saturated Fat: <1 g, Protein: 2 g, Carbohydrate: 11 g, Cholesterol: 1 mg, Sodium: 225 mg, Fiber: 2 g, Iron: <1 mg, Calcium: 26 mg, Vitamin A: 392 RE, Vitamin C: 43 mg, Sugar: 4 g
Dietary Exchanges: 2 Vegetable

Sausage Vegetable Rotini Soup

6 ounces bulk sausage
1 cup chopped yellow
    onion
1 cup chopped green bell
    pepper
3 cups water
1 can (14½ ounces) diced
    tomatoes, undrained

¼ cup ketchup
2 teaspoons reduced-
    sodium beef granules
2 teaspoons chili powder
4 ounces uncooked
    tri-colored rotini
1 cup frozen corn kernels,
    thawed

Heat Dutch oven over medium-high heat until hot. Coat with nonstick cooking spray. Add sausage and cook 3 minutes or until no longer pink, breaking up sausage into small pieces. Add onion and pepper; cook 3 to 4 minutes or until onion is translucent.

Add water, tomatoes with liquid, ketchup, beef granules and chili powder; bring to a boil over high heat. Stir in pasta and return to a boil. Reduce heat to medium-low and simmer, uncovered, 12 minutes. Stir in corn and cook 2 minutes.

Makes 4 servings (6½ cups)

Nutrients per Serving: Calories: 220, Calories from Fat: 28%, Total Fat: 7 g, Saturated Fat: 2 g, Protein: 10 g, Carbohydrate: 32 g, Cholesterol: 17 mg, Sodium: 393 mg, Fiber: 4 g, Iron: 1 mg, Calcium: 28 mg, Vitamin A: 118 RE, Vitamin C: 73 mg, Sugar: 6 g
Dietary Exchanges: 2 Starch, 1 Meat, ½ Fat

Corn is a low-fat complex carbohydrate, a healthy addition to any dish. Corn is high in fiber and a good source of several vitamins, including vitamin C.

Sausage Vegetable Rotini Soup

Main DISHES

Ravioli with Tomato Pesto

4 ounces frozen cheese
    ravioli
1¼ cups coarsely chopped
    plum tomatoes
¼ cup fresh basil leaves
2 teaspoons pine nuts

2 teaspoons olive oil
¼ teaspoon salt
⅛ teaspoon black pepper
1 tablespoon grated
    Parmesan cheese

1. Cook ravioli according to package directions; drain.

2. Meanwhile, combine tomatoes, basil, pine nuts, oil, salt and pepper in food processor. Process using on/off pulsing action just until ingredients are chopped. Serve over ravioli. Top with cheese.

Makes 2 servings

Nutrients per Serving: Calories: 175, Calories from Fat: 34%, Total Fat: 10 g, Saturated Fat: 2 g, Protein: 10 g, Carbohydrate: 20 g, Cholesterol: 59 mg, Sodium: 459 mg, Fiber: 3 g, Iron: 2 mg, Calcium: 119 mg, Vitamin A: 116 RE, Vitamin C: 27 mg, Sugar: 5 g
Dietary Exchanges: 1 Vegetable, 1 Starch, 1 Meat, ½ Fat

Ravioli with Tomato Pesto

Grilled Honey Garlic Pork Chops

¼ cup lemon juice

¼ cup honey

2 tablespoons soy sauce

1 tablespoon dry sherry

2 cloves garlic, minced

4 boneless center-cut lean pork chops (about 4 ounces each)

Combine all ingredients except pork chops in small bowl. Place pork in shallow baking dish; pour marinade over pork. Cover and refrigerate 4 hours or overnight. Remove pork from marinade. Heat remaining marinade in small saucepan over medium heat to a simmer. Grill pork over medium-hot coals 12 to 15 minutes, turning once during cooking and basting frequently with marinade, until meat thermometer registers 155 to 160°F.

Makes 4 servings

Favorite recipe from **National Honey Board**

Nutrients per Serving: Calories: 281, Calories from Fat: 34%, Total Fat: 11 g, Saturated Fat: 4 g, Protein: 25 g, Carbohydrate: 20 g, Cholesterol: 54 mg, Sodium: 570 mg, Fiber: <1 g, Iron: 2 mg, Calcium: 34 mg, Vitamin A: 2 RE, Vitamin C: 8 mg, Sugar: 19 g
Dietary Exchanges: 1½ Starch, 3 Meat

Lean pork chops are a terrific source of protein, B vitamins and zinc. They are easy to prepare and adapt well to a wide variety of flavors and cooking methods.

Grilled Honey Garlic Pork Chop

Caribbean Sea Bass with Mango Salsa

Prep Time: 10 minutes   **Cook Time:** 8 minutes

4 (4 ounces each) skinless
sea bass fillets, about
1 inch thick
1 teaspoon Caribbean jerk
seasoning
Nonstick cooking spray
1 ripe mango, peeled,
pitted and diced, *or*
1 cup diced drained
bottled mango

2 tablespoons chopped
fresh cilantro
2 teaspoons fresh lime
juice
1 teaspoon minced fresh or
bottled jalapeño
pepper*

*Jalapeño peppers can sting and irritate the skin; wear rubber gloves when handling peppers and do not touch eyes. Wash hands after handling peppers.

1. Prepare grill or preheat broiler. Sprinkle fish with seasoning; coat lightly with cooking spray. Grill fish over medium coals or broil 5 inches from heat for 4 to 5 minutes per side or until fish flakes easily with fork.

2. Meanwhile, combine mango, cilantro, lime juice and jalapeño pepper; mix well. Serve over fish.   *Makes 4 servings*

Nutrients per Serving: Calories: 146, Calories from Fat: 15%, Total Fat: 2 g, Saturated Fat: 1 g, Protein: 21 g, Carbohydrate: 9 g, Cholesterol: 47 mg, Sodium: 189 mg, Fiber: 1 g, Sugar: 8 g
Dietary Exchanges: ½ Fruit, 2 Meat

Caribbean Sea Bass with
Mango Salsa

Tex-Mex Tostadas

4 (8-inch) fat-free flour
    tortillas
Nonstick cooking spray
1 green bell pepper, diced
¾ pound boneless skinless
    chicken breast, cut into
    strips
1½ teaspoons fresh or
    bottled minced garlic
1 teaspoon chili powder

1 teaspoon ground cumin
½ cup chunky salsa,
    divided
⅓ cup sliced green onions
1 cup canned fat-free
    refried beans
1 medium tomato, diced
¼ cup fat-free or reduced-
    fat sour cream
    (optional)

1. Preheat oven to 450°F. Place tortillas on baking sheet; coat both sides with cooking spray. Bake 5 minutes or until lightly browned and crisp. Remove; set aside.

2. Coat large nonstick skillet with cooking spray. Add bell pepper; cook and stir 4 minutes. Add chicken, garlic, chili powder and cumin; cook and stir 4 minutes or until chicken is no longer pink in center. Add ¼ cup salsa and green onions; cook and stir 1 minute. Remove skillet from heat; set aside.

3. Combine refried beans and remaining ¼ cup salsa in a microwavable bowl. Cook uncovered at HIGH 1½ minutes or until beans are heated through.

4. Spread bean mixture evenly over tortillas. Spoon chicken mixture and tomato over bean mixture. Garnish with sour cream, if desired.

Makes 4 servings

Nutrients per Serving: Calories: 251, Calories from Fat: 9%, Total Fat: 3 g, Saturated Fat: 1 g, Protein: 26 g, Carbohydrate: 30 g, Cholesterol: 52 mg, Sodium: 707 mg, Fiber: 11 g, Iron: 2 mg, Calcium: 66 mg, Vitamin A: 79 RE, Vitamin C: 24 mg, Sugar: 4 g
Dietary Exchanges: 2 Starch, 2 Meat

Campbell's® Healthy Request®
Primavera Fish Fillets

Prep Time: 10 minutes   **Cook Time:** 20 minutes

1 large carrot, cut into matchstick-thin strips (about 1 cup)

2 stalks celery, cut into matchstick-thin strips (about 1 cup)

1 small onion, diced (about ¼ cup)

¼ cup water

2 tablespoons Chablis *or* other dry white wine

½ teaspoon dried thyme leaves, crushed
Generous dash pepper

1 can (10¾ ounces) CAMPBELL'S® HEALTHY REQUEST® Condensed Cream of Mushroom Soup

1 pound firm white fish fillets (cod, haddock or halibut)

1. In medium skillet mix carrot, celery, onion, water, wine, thyme and pepper. Over medium-high heat, heat to a boil. Reduce heat to low. Cover and cook 5 minutes or until vegetables are tender-crisp.

2. Stir in soup. Over medium heat, heat to a boil.

3. Place fish in soup mixture. Reduce heat to low. Cover and cook 5 minutes or until fish flakes easily when tested with a fork.

Makes 4 servings

Note: In this recipe, CAMPBELL'S® HEALTHY REQUEST® creates a lower fat alternative to a traditional Newburg-style sauce made with butter and cream.

Nutrients per Serving: Calories: 161, Calories from Fat: 14%, Total Fat: 3 g, Saturated Fat: 1 g, Protein: 21 g, Carbohydrate: 11 g, Cholesterol: 55 mg, Sodium: 398 mg, Fiber: 1 g, Iron: 1 mg, Calcium: 97 mg, Vitamin A: 522 RE, Vitamin C: 5 mg, Sugar: 3 g
Dietary Exchanges: ½ Starch, 3 Meat

Asian Beef Wraps

1 cup UNCLE BEN'S®
   Instant Rice
8 (6-inch) soft flour tortillas
2 teaspoons seasoned
   stir-fry oil
½ pound thin boneless beef
   sirloin steak, cut into
   2-inch strips

½ package (16 ounces)
   frozen stir-fry peppers
   and onions
¼ cup stir-fry sauce
2 tablespoons water
¼ cup thinly sliced green
   onions

1. Cook rice according to package directions; keep warm.

2. Heat tortillas according to package directions; keep warm.

3. Heat oil in large skillet over medium-high heat until hot. Add beef; stir-fry 4 minutes or until no longer pink.

4. Add peppers and onions; stir-fry 1 minute. Stir in stir-fry sauce and water. Reduce heat and simmer gently 6 minutes, stirring frequently. Remove from heat.

5. Place ¼ cup cooked rice in center of each tortilla; top with ¼ cup beef mixture and about 1½ teaspoons green onions. Fold in both sides of tortilla; roll up tightly from bottom, keeping filling firmly packed. Slice each wrap diagonally into pieces.

Makes 4 servings

Serving Suggestion: Chopped peanuts can be sprinkled over the beef filling with the green onions, if desired.

Nutrients per Serving: Calories: 436, Calories from Fat: 20%, Total Fat: 10 g, Saturated Fat: 2 g, Protein: 19 g, Carbohydrate: 66 g, Cholesterol: 30 mg, Sodium: 898 mg, Fiber: 4 g, Iron: 4 mg, Calcium: 98 mg, Vitamin A: 1 RE, Vitamin C: 1 mg, Sugar: 4 g
Dietary Exchanges: 1 Vegetable, 4 Starch, 1 Meat, 1½ Fat

Grilled Fish with Orange-Chile Salsa

3 medium oranges, peeled and sectioned* (about 1¼ cups segments)
¼ cup finely diced green, red or yellow bell pepper
3 tablespoons chopped cilantro, divided
3 tablespoons lime juice, divided
1 tablespoon honey
1 teaspoon minced, seeded serrano pepper *or* 1 tablespoon minced jalapeño pepper
1¼ pounds firm white fish fillets, such as orange roughy, lingcod, halibut or red snapper
Lime slices
Zucchini ribbons, cooked

*Canned mandarin orange segments can be substituted for fresh orange segments, if desired.

To prepare Orange-Chile Salsa, combine orange segments, bell pepper, 2 tablespoons cilantro, 2 tablespoons lime juice, honey and serrano pepper. Set aside.

Season fish fillets with remaining 1 tablespoon cilantro and 1 tablespoon lime juice. Lightly oil grid to prevent sticking. Grill fish on covered grill over medium KINGSFORD® Briquets 5 minutes. Turn and top with lime slices, if desired. Grill about 5 minutes until fish flakes easily when tested with fork. Serve with Orange-Chile Salsa. Garnish with zucchini ribbons.

Makes 4 servings

Note: Allow about 10 minutes grilling time per inch thickness of fish fillets.

Nutrients per Serving: Calories: 154, Calories from Fat: 7%, Total Fat: 1 g, Saturated Fat: <1 g, Protein: 21 g, Carbohydrate: 14 g, Cholesterol: 28 mg, Sodium: 88 mg, Fiber: <1 g, Iron: 1 mg, Calcium: 55 mg, Vitamin A: 59 RE, Vitamin C: 57 mg, Sugar: 13 g
Dietary Exchanges: 1 Fruit, 3 Meat

Grilled Fish with Orange-Chile Salsa

Chicken & Beans with Pasta

Preparation Time: 15 minutes   **Cook Time:** 25 minutes
Total Time: 40 minutes

½ pound boneless, skinless chicken breasts, cut into bite-size strips
1 small carrot, chopped
½ cup chopped onion
⅓ cup thinly sliced celery
2 cloves garlic, finely chopped
2 tablespoons FLEISCHMANN'S® Original Margarine

1 (14-ounce) can whole peeled tomatoes, coarsely chopped
½ cup canned cannellini beans, drained
8 ounces bow-tie pasta, cooked and drained
Fresh chopped parsley and grated Parmesan cheese, optional

1. Cook and stir chicken, carrot, onion, celery and garlic in margarine in large skillet over medium-high heat until chicken is no longer pink and vegetables are tender.

2. Add tomatoes and beans; reduce heat and cook for 15 minutes.

3. Toss bean mixture with hot cooked pasta. Garnish with parsley and cheese if desired.   *Makes 4 servings*

Nutrients per Serving: Calories: 398, Calories from Fat: 23%, Total Fat: 10 g, Saturated Fat: 2 g, Protein: 23 g, Carbohydrate: 52 g, Cholesterol: 100 mg, Sodium: 320 mg, Fiber: 4 g, Iron: 3 mg, Calcium: 61 mg, Vitamin A: 570 RE, Vitamin C: 18 mg, Sugar: 6 g
Dietary Exchanges: 1 Vegetable, 3 Starch, 2 Meat, 1 Fat

Cannellini beans are large white Italian kidney beans. Great Northern beans may be used as a substitute if cannellini are unavailable.

Bandstand Chili

Preparation Time: 25 minutes

2 cups chopped cooked
   BUTTERBALL® Boneless
   Young Turkey
1 tablespoon vegetable oil
1½ cups chopped onions
1½ cups chopped red bell
   peppers
2 tablespoons mild
   Mexican seasoning*

1 clove garlic, minced
1 can (28 ounces) tomato
   purée with tomato bits
1 can (15½ ounces) light
   red kidney beans,
   undrained

*To make your own Mexican seasoning, combine 1 tablespoon chili powder, 1½ teaspoons oregano and 1½ teaspoons cumin.

Heat oil in large skillet over medium heat until hot. Add onions, bell peppers, Mexican seasoning and garlic. Cook and stir 4 to 5 minutes. Add tomato purée and beans; stir in turkey. Reduce heat to low; simmer 5 minutes. *Makes 8 servings*

Nutrients per Serving: Calories: 179, Calories from Fat: 22%, Total Fat: 5 g, Saturated Fat: 1 g, Protein: 16 g, Carbohydrate: 21 g, Cholesterol: 27 mg, Sodium: 385 mg, Fiber: 7 g, Iron: 3 mg, Calcium: 81 mg, Vitamin A: 95 RE, Vitamin C: 38 mg, Sugar: 8 g
Dietary Exchanges: 1 Vegetable, 1 Starch, 1½ Meat

Speedy Spaghetti with Sausage

12 ounces whole wheat spaghetti

8 ounces hot Italian turkey sausage

1 cup chopped onion

3 cloves garlic, minced

1 can (28 ounces) crushed or puréed tomatoes, undrained

1 can (14½ ounces) no-salt-added stewed tomatoes, undrained

1 teaspoon dried basil leaves

¼ teaspoon red pepper flakes (optional)

1 large or 2 medium zucchini or yellow squash, cut into chunks

¼ cup grated Parmesan cheese

1. Cook spaghetti according to package directions, omitting salt. Drain and set aside.

2. Meanwhile, crumble sausage into large saucepan, discarding casings. Add onion and garlic. Cook over medium heat until sausage is no longer pink, stirring occasionally; drain, if needed.

3. Add crushed tomatoes, stewed tomatoes, basil and pepper flakes, if desired; bring to a simmer. Stir in zucchini; return to a simmer and cook, uncovered, 15 minutes or until zucchini is tender and sauce thickens, stirring occasionally.

4. Top cooked pasta with meat sauce; sprinkle with cheese.

Makes 6 servings

Nutrients per Serving: Calories: 331, Calories from Fat: 16%, Total Fat: 6 g, Saturated Fat: 2 g, Protein: 19 g, Carbohydrate: 54 g, Cholesterol: 23 mg, Sodium: 708 mg, Fiber: 10 g
Dietary Exchanges: 2 Vegetable, 3 Starch, 1 Meat, ½ Fat

Speedy Spaghetti with Sausage

Margarita Pork Kabobs

1 cup margarita drink mix
    or 1 cup lime juice,
    4 teaspoons sugar and
    ½ teaspoon salt
1 teaspoon ground
    coriander
1 clove garlic, minced
1 pound pork tenderloin,
    cut into 1-inch cubes
2 tablespoons margarine,
    softened

2 teaspoons lime juice
1 tablespoon minced fresh
    parsley
⅛ teaspoon sugar
1 large green or red bell
    pepper, cut into 1-inch
    cubes
2 ears corn, cut into
    8 pieces

For marinade, combine margarita mix, coriander and garlic in small bowl. Place pork cubes in large resealable plastic food storage bag; pour marinade over pork. Close bag securely; turn to coat. Marinate for at least 30 minutes. Combine margarine, lime juice, parsley and sugar in small bowl; set aside. Thread pork cubes onto four skewers, alternating with pieces of bell pepper and corn. (If using bamboo skewers, soak in water 20 to 30 minutes before using to prevent them from burning.) Grill over hot coals for 15 to 20 minutes or until barely pink in center, basting with margarine mixture and turning frequently.   *Makes 4 servings*

Favorite recipe from **National Pork Producers Council**

Nutrients per Serving: Calories: 240, Calories from Fat: 37%, Total Fat: 10 g, Saturated Fat: 3 g, Protein: 25 g, Carbohydrate: 13 g, Cholesterol: 66 mg, Sodium: 129 mg, Fiber: 1 g, Iron: 2 mg, Calcium: 12 mg, Vitamin A: 82 RE, Vitamin C: 21 mg, Sugar: 5 g
Dietary Exchanges: 1 Starch, 3 Meat

Margarita Pork Kabobs

Tangy Italian Chicken Sandwiches

Prep Time: 15 minutes

2 cups (8 ounces) chopped cooked chicken or turkey breast

⅓ cup drained bottled hot or mild pickled vegetables (jardinière)

2 ounces reduced-fat provolone cheese slices, diced

¼ cup chopped fresh parsley

3 tablespoons reduced-fat Italian salad dressing

¼ teaspoon dried oregano

4 pita breads

8 leaves romaine or red leaf lettuce

1. Combine chicken, pickled vegetables, cheese, parsley, dressing and oregano in medium bowl; mix well.

2. Cut pitas in half. Line each pocket with lettuce leaf and fill with ⅛ chicken mixture.   *Makes 4 servings*

Nutrients per Serving: Calories: 330, Calories from Fat: 20%, Total Fat: 7 g, Saturated Fat: 3 g, Protein: 28 g, Carbohydrate: 39 g, Cholesterol: 53 mg, Sodium: 610 mg, Fiber: 6 g, Sugar: 5 g
Dietary Exchanges: 2½ Starch, 2 Meat, ½ Fat

Provolone cheese originated in Southern Italy; it has a firm texture and a mild, smoky flavor that is very popular in sandwiches and on pizzas.

Tangy Italian Chicken Sandwich

Vegetables & SIDES

Roasted Butternut Squash

1 pound butternut squash, peeled and cut into 1-inch cubes

2 medium onions, coarsely chopped

8 ounces carrots, peeled and cut into ½-inch diagonal slices (about 2 cups)

1 tablespoon dark brown sugar

¼ teaspoon salt
 Black pepper to taste

1 tablespoon butter or margarine, melted

Preheat oven to 400°F. Line large baking sheet with foil and coat with nonstick cooking spray. Arrange vegetables in single layer on foil; coat lightly with cooking spray. Sprinkle vegetables with brown sugar, salt and pepper.

Bake 30 minutes. Stir gently; bake 10 to 15 minutes longer or until vegetables are tender. Remove from oven; drizzle with butter and toss to coat.   *Makes 5 (1-cup) servings*

Nutrients per Serving: Calories: 143, Calories from Fat: 16%, Total Fat: 3 g, Saturated Fat: 2 g, Protein: 3 g, Carbohydrate: 30 g, Cholesterol: 7 mg, Sodium: 167 mg, Fiber: 8 g, Iron: 1 mg, Calcium: 96 mg, Vitamin A: 2446 RE, Vitamin C: 33 mg, Sugar: 13 g
Dietary Exchanges: 1 Vegetable, 1½ Starch, ½ Fat

Roasted Butternut Squash

Sweet Potato and Apple Casserole

Preparation Time: 20 minutes

3 medium sweet potatoes
3 medium apples
¼ cup sugar
1 tablespoon grated
    orange peel

½ teaspoon ground nutmeg
¼ teaspoon salt
¼ cup orange juice

Microwave sweet potatoes on HIGH 8 minutes. Peel and cut into ½-inch slices. Peel and core apples; slice crosswise into ½-inch rings. Combine sugar, orange peel, nutmeg and salt in small bowl. Alternate slices of sweet potatoes and apples in deep 1½-quart casserole. Sprinkle sugar mixture over each layer. Add orange juice and cover. Microwave on HIGH 6 minutes.   *Makes 6 servings*

Favorite recipe from **New York Apple Association, Inc.**

Nutrients per Serving: Calories: 138, Calories from Fat: 2%, Total Fat: <1 g, Saturated Fat: <1 g, Protein: 1 g, Carbohydrate: 34 g, Cholesterol: 0 mg, Sodium: 103 mg, Fiber: 4 g, Iron: <1 mg, Calcium: 24 mg, Vitamin A: 1249 RE, Vitamin C: 25 mg, Sugar: 25 g
Dietary Exchanges: 2 Fruit

Rich in vitamin A, vitamin C and minerals, sweet potatoes pack more nutrition than white potatoes. Their sweetness is due to a remarkably high sugar content that is increased even further during cooking.

Campbell's® Healthy Request® Creamy Risotto

Prep Time: 5 minutes   **Cook/Stand Time:** 15 minutes

1 can (10¾ ounces) CAMPBELL'S® HEALTHY REQUEST® Condensed Cream of Mushroom Soup

1½ cups CAMPBELL'S® HEALTHY REQUEST® Ready to Serve Chicken Broth

1½ cups uncooked Minute® Original Rice

1 tablespoon grated Parmesan cheese

Pepper

1. In medium saucepan mix soup and broth. Over medium-high heat, heat to a boil.

2. Stir in rice and cheese. Cover and remove from heat. Let stand 10 minutes. Fluff with fork. Serve with freshly ground pepper and additional cheese if desired.   *Makes 4 servings*

Tomato-Basil Risotto: In step 2, add 1 tablespoon chopped fresh basil *or* ¼ teaspoon dried basil leaves, crushed, and 1 small tomato, diced (about ½ cup) *or* ½ cup drained cut-up canned tomatoes with rice.

Confetti Risotto: In step 1 add ¼ teaspoon dried thyme leaves, crushed, ½ cup frozen peas, 1 small carrot, shredded (about ⅓ cup) and 1 small onion, finely chopped (about ¼ cup) with soup and broth. Proceed with step 2.

Tip: Use HEALTHY REQUEST® to lighten up your favorite dishes such as this international specialty—easily and deliciously.

Nutrients per Serving: Calories: 188, Calories from Fat: 5%, Total Fat: 1 g, Saturated Fat: <1 g, Protein: 6 g, Carbohydrate: 38 g, Cholesterol: 1 mg, Sodium: 387 mg, Fiber: 2 g, Iron: 1 mg, Calcium: 31 mg, Vitamin A: 2 RE, Vitamin C: <1 mg, Sugar: <1 g
Dietary Exchanges: 2½ Starch

Low-Calorie Mashed Potatoes

2 pounds medium red
   boiling potatoes,
   peeled and cut into
   chunks
4 large cloves garlic,
   peeled

¾ cup buttermilk (1½% fat)
½ teaspoon salt
¼ teaspoon black pepper
2 tablespoons chopped
   chives for garnish

1. Place potatoes and garlic in large saucepan. Add enough water to cover; bring to a boil over high heat. Reduce heat and simmer, uncovered, 20 to 30 minutes or until potatoes are fork-tender. Drain.

2. Place potatoes and garlic in medium bowl. Mash with potato masher or beat with electric mixer at medium speed until smooth.*

3. Add buttermilk, salt and pepper. Stir with fork until just combined. Garnish, if desired. *Makes 8 servings*

*For a smoother texture, force potatoes through potato ricer or food mill into medium bowl. Finish as directed in step 3.

Nutrients per Serving: Calories: 101, Calories from Fat: 3%, Total Fat: <1 g, Saturated Fat: <1 g, Protein: 3 g, Carbohydrate: 22 g, Cholesterol: 1 mg, Sodium: 175 mg, Fiber: 2 g, Calcium: 39 mg, Vitamin A: 5 RE, Vitamin C: 9 mg, Sugar: 1 g
Dietary Exchanges: 1½ Starch

Low-Calorie Mashed Potatoes

Glazed Maple Acorn Squash

1 large acorn or golden
acorn squash
¼ cup water
2 tablespoons pure maple
syrup

1 tablespoon margarine or
butter, melted
¼ teaspoon ground
cinnamon

1. Preheat oven to 375°F.

2. Cut stem and blossom ends from squash. Cut squash crosswise into four equal slices. Discard seeds and membrane. Place water in 13×9-inch baking dish. Arrange squash in dish; cover with foil. Bake 30 minutes or until tender.

3. Combine syrup, margarine and cinnamon in small bowl; mix well. Uncover squash; pour off water. Brush squash with syrup mixture, letting excess pool in center of squash. Return to oven; bake 10 minutes or until syrup mixture is bubbly

Makes 4 servings

Nutrients per Serving: Calories: 161, Calories from Fat: 16%, Total Fat: 3 g, Saturated Fat: 2 g, Protein: 2 g, Carbohydrate: 35 g, Cholesterol: 8 mg, Sodium: 39 mg, Fiber: 4 g, Sugar: 14 g
Dietary Exchanges: 2 Starch, ½ Fat

Orange Sesame Couscous

1 cup fresh orange juice
(3 SUNKIST® oranges)
½ cup chopped red or
green bell pepper
1 teaspoon sesame oil
⅛ teaspoon salt

⅔ cup uncooked couscous
1 SUNKIST® orange, peeled
and cut into bite-size
pieces
3 tablespoons chopped
green onions

In medium saucepan, combine orange juice, bell pepper, sesame oil and salt. Bring just to a boil; stir in couscous. Cover and remove from heat. Let stand 5 minutes. Stir with fork to fluff up mixture. Stir in orange and green onions. *Makes 3 (1-cup) servings*

Nutrients per Serving: Calories: 236, Calories from Fat: 8%, Total Fat: 2 g, Saturated Fat: <1 g, Protein: 7 g, Carbohydrate: 48 g, Cholesterol: 0 mg, Sodium: 103 mg, Fiber: 4 g, Iron: 1 mg, Calcium: 42 mg, Vitamin A: 51 RE, Vitamin C: 99 mg, Sugar: 14 g
Dietary Exchanges: 1 Fruit, 2 Starch, ½ Fat

Glazed Maple Acorn Squash

Vegetable Fried Rice

1 teaspoon vegetable oil
1½ cups small broccoli florets
½ cup chopped red bell
    pepper
2 cups chilled cooked white
    rice

1 tablespoon low-sodium
    soy sauce
½ cup shredded carrot

1. Heat oil in large nonstick skillet over medium heat. Add broccoli and bell pepper; stir-fry 3 minutes or until crisp-tender.

2. Add rice and soy sauce; stir-fry 2 minutes. Add carrot; heat through. Serve rice mixture on kale-lined plates.

Makes 4 side-dish servings

Tip: Don't throw away those broccoli stems after removing the florets for this recipe. Instead, peel the stems with a vegetable peeler, cut them crosswise into thin slices and steam until crisp-tender.

Nutrients per Serving: Calories: 193, Calories from Fat: 8%, Total Fat: 2 g, Saturated Fat: <1 g, Protein: 5 g, Carbohydrate: 40 g, Cholesterol: 0 mg, Sodium: 278 mg, Fiber: 5 g, Iron: 2 mg, Calcium: 47 mg, Vitamin A: 526 RE, Vitamin C: 143 mg
Dietary Exchanges: 2 Vegetable, 2 Starch

Broccoli floret are packed with nutrients, including vitamin C, vitamin A, calcium and fiber. Quick stir-frying or steaming are excellent ways to retain these nutrients. (Many nutrients are lost when vegetables are boiled.)

Vegetable Fried Rice

Oven French Fries

4 medium potatoes
1 tablespoon CRISCO® Oil*
½ teaspoon celery salt

⅛ teaspoon garlic powder
⅛ teaspoon pepper
⅛ teaspoon paprika

*Use your favorite Crisco Oil product.

1. Heat oven to 425°F. Place cooling rack on countertop.

2. Peel potatoes. Cut into long ½-inch strips. Dry with paper towels. Place in large bowl. Add oil. Toss to coat. Place potatoes in single layer on unprepared baking sheet.

3. Combine celery salt, garlic powder, pepper and paprika in small bowl. Sprinkle potatoes with half of seasoning mixture. Turn potatoes over. Sprinkle with remaining seasoning mixture.

4. Bake at 425°F for 25 to 30 minutes or until potatoes are tender and evenly browned, turning occasionally. *Do not overbake.* Remove baking sheet to cooling rack. Serve warm.

Makes 6 servings

Nutrients per Serving: Calories: 98, Calories from Fat: 22%, Total Fat: 2 g, Saturated Fat: <1 g, Protein: 2 g, Carbohydrate: 18 g, Cholesterol: 0 mg, Sodium: 175 mg, Fiber: 2 g,
Iron: <1 mg, Calcium: 9 mg, Vitamin A: 4 RE, Vitamin C: 7 mg, Sugar: 2 g
Dietary Exchanges: 1 Starch, ½ Fat

Moroccan Couscous

Prep Time: 5 minutes   **Cook Time:** 10 minutes

1 cup low-sodium chicken
   broth
½ teaspoon ground
   cinnamon
⅛ teaspoon ground nutmeg
⅔ cup uncooked couscous
⅔ cup DOLE® Pitted Dates or
   Pitted Prunes, chopped
½ cup chopped green

   onions
⅓ cup DOLE® Golden or
   Seedless Raisins
3 tablespoons sliced
   almonds, toasted

• Combine broth, cinnamon and nutmeg in medium saucepan. Bring to boil.

• Stir in couscous, dates, green onions and raisins. Remove from heat; cover. Let stand 5 minutes.

• Stir couscous mixture with fork; spoon into serving dish. Sprinkle with almonds.

Makes 6 servings

Nutrients per Serving: Calories: 195, Calories from Fat: 11%, Total Fat: 2 g, Saturated Fat: <1 g, Protein: 4 g, Carbohydrate: 39 g, Cholesterol: 0 mg, Sodium: 11 mg, Fiber: 3 g, Calcium: 21 mg, Vitamin A: 3 RE, Vitamin C: 1 mg, Sugar: 19 g
Dietary Exchanges: ½ Fruit, 2 Starch, ½ Fat

In addition to being able to satisfy a sweet tooth, dates are also loaded with fiber, potassium and other vitamins and minerals. They're a great addition to both savory and sweet recipes.

Pepper and Squash Gratin

12 ounces russet potato, unpeeled

8 ounces yellow squash, thinly sliced

8 ounces zucchini, thinly sliced

2 cups frozen pepper stir-fry, thawed

1 teaspoon dried oregano leaves

½ teaspoon salt

Black pepper to taste

½ cup grated Parmesan cheese or shredded reduced-fat sharp Cheddar cheese

1 tablespoon butter or margarine, cut into 8 pieces

Preheat oven to 375°F. Coat 12×8-inch glass baking dish with nonstick cooking spray. Pierce potato several times with fork. Microwave at HIGH (100%) 3 minutes; cut into thin slices.

Layer half of potatoes, yellow squash, zucchini, pepper stir-fry, oregano, salt, black pepper and cheese in prepared baking dish. Repeat layers and top with butter. Cover tightly with foil; bake 25 minutes or until vegetables are just tender. Remove foil and bake 10 minutes longer or until lightly browned.

Makes 8 servings

Nutrients per Serving: Calories: 106, Calories from Fat: 26%, Total Fat: 3 g, Saturated Fat: 2 g, Protein: 4 g, Carbohydrate: 15 g, Cholesterol: 8 mg, Sodium: 267 mg, Fiber: 2 g, Iron: <1 mg, Calcium: 79 mg, Vitamin A: 34 RE, Vitamin C: 10 mg, Sugar: 3 g
Dietary Exchanges: 1 Starch, ½ Fat

Pepper and Squash Gratin

Orzo with Spinach and Red Pepper

4 ounces uncooked orzo

1 teaspoon olive oil

1 medium red bell pepper, diced

3 cloves garlic, minced

1 package (10 ounces) frozen chopped spinach, thawed and squeezed dry

¼ cup grated Parmesan cheese

½ teaspoon minced fresh oregano or basil (optional)

¼ teaspoon lemon pepper

1. Prepare orzo according to package directions; drain well and set aside.

2. Spray large nonstick skillet with nonstick cooking spray. Heat skillet over medium-high heat until hot and add oil, tilting skillet to coat bottom. Add bell pepper and garlic; cook and stir 2 to 3 minutes or until bell pepper is crisp-tender. Add orzo and spinach; stir until evenly mixed and heated through. Remove from heat and stir in Parmesan cheese, oregano, if desired, and lemon pepper. Garnish as desired. *Makes 6 servings*

Nutrients per Serving: Calories: 116, Calories from Fat: 19%, Total Fat: 3 g, Saturated Fat: 1 g, Protein: 6 g, Carbohydrate: 19 g, Cholesterol: 3 mg, Sodium: 152 mg, Fiber: 2 g, Iron: 2 mg, Calcium: 115 mg, Vitamin A: 493 RE, Vitamin C: 89 mg
Dietary Exchanges: 1 Vegetable, 1 Starch, ½ Fat

Orzo with Spinach and Red Pepper

Guilt-Free DESSERTS

Brownie Cake Delight

1 package reduced-fat
   fudge brownie mix
⅓ cup strawberry all-fruit
   spread
2 cups thawed reduced-fat
   nondairy whipped
   topping

¼ teaspoon almond extract
2 cups strawberries, stems
   removed, halved
¼ cup chocolate sauce

Prepare brownies according to package directions, substituting 11×7-inch baking pan. Cool completely in pan. Whisk fruit spread in small bowl until smooth. Combine whipped topping and almond extract in medium bowl.

Cut brownie crosswise in half. Place half of brownie, cut side down, on serving dish. Spread with fruit spread and 1 cup whipped topping. Place second half of brownie, cut side down, over bottom layer. Spread with remaining whipped topping. Arrange strawberries on whipped topping. Drizzle chocolate sauce onto cake before serving. *Makes 16 servings*

Nutrients per Serving: Calories: 193, Calories from Fat: 14%, Total Fat: 3 g, Saturated Fat: <1 g, Protein: 2 g, Carbohydrate: 41 g, Cholesterol: <1 mg, Sodium: 140 mg, Fiber: <1 g, Iron: 1 mg, Calcium: 11 mg, Vitamin A: 11 RE, Vitamin C: 11 mg
Dietary Exchanges: ½ Fruit, 2 Starch, ½ Fat

Brownie Cake Delight

Apricot Biscotti

3 cups all-purpose flour
1½ teaspoons baking soda
½ teaspoon salt
3 eggs
⅔ cup sugar
1 teaspoon vanilla

½ cup chopped dried
  apricots*
⅓ cup sliced almonds,
  chopped
1 tablespoon reduced-fat
  (2%) milk

*Other chopped dried fruits, such as dried cherries, cranberries or blueberries, may be substituted.

1. Preheat oven to 350°F. Lightly coat cookie sheet with nonstick cooking spray; set aside.

2. Combine flour, baking soda and salt in medium bowl; set aside.

3. Beat eggs, sugar and vanilla in large bowl with electric mixer at medium speed until combined. Add flour mixture; beat well.

4. Stir in apricots and almonds. Turn dough out onto lightly floured work surface. Knead 4 to 6 times. Roll dough into 20-inch log; place on prepared cookie sheet. Brush dough with milk.

5. Bake 30 minutes or until firm to touch. Remove from oven; cool 10 minutes. Diagonally slice into 30 biscotti. Place slices on cookie sheet. Bake 10 minutes; turn and bake an additional 10 minutes. Cool on wire racks. Store in airtight container.

Makes 30 servings

Nutrients per Serving: Calories: 86, Calories from Fat: 10%, Total Fat: 1 g, Saturated Fat: <1 g, Protein: 2 g, Carbohydrate: 16 g, Cholesterol: 21 mg, Sodium: 108 mg, Fiber: 1 g
Dietary Exchanges: 1 Starch

Apricot Biscotti

Rustic Apple Croustade

1⅓ cups all-purpose flour
¼ teaspoon salt
2 tablespoons margarine
  or butter
2 tablespoons vegetable
  shortening
4 to 5 tablespoons ice
  water
⅓ cup packed light brown
  sugar

1 tablespoon cornstarch
1 teaspoon cinnamon,
  divided
3 large Jonathan or
  MacIntosh apples,
  peeled, cored and
  thinly sliced (4 cups)
1 egg white, beaten
1 tablespoon granulated
  sugar

1. Combine flour and salt in small bowl. Cut in margarine and shortening with pastry blender or two knives until mixture resembles coarse crumbs. Mix in ice water, 1 tablespoon at a time, until mixture comes together and forms a soft dough. Wrap in plastic wrap; refrigerate 30 minutes.

2. Preheat oven to 375°F. Roll out pastry on floured surface to ⅛-inch thickness. Cut into 12-inch circle. Transfer pastry to nonstick jelly-roll pan.

3. Combine brown sugar, cornstarch and ¾ teaspoon cinnamon in medium bowl; mix well. Add apples; toss well. Spoon apple mixture into center of pastry, leaving a 1½-inch border. Fold pastry over apples, folding edges in gently and pressing down lightly. Brush egg white over pastry. Combine remaining ¼ teaspoon cinnamon and granulated sugar in small bowl; sprinkle evenly over tart.

4. Bake 35 to 40 minutes or until apples are tender and crust is golden brown. Let stand 20 minutes before serving. Cut into wedges.

Makes 8 serving

Nutrients per Serving: Calories: 213, Calories from Fat: 26%, Total Fat: 6 g, Saturated Fat: 1 g, Protein: 3 g, Carbohydrate: 37 g, Cholesterol: 0 mg, Sodium: 118 mg, Fiber: 3 g, Iron: 1 mg, Calcium: 22 mg, Vitamin A: 33 RE, Vitamin C: <1 mg, Sugar: 10 g
Dietary Exchanges: 1½ Fruit, 1 Starch, 1½ Fat

Rustic Apple Croustade

Chocolate Fruit Crispies

6 cups crisp rice cereal
½ cup raisins
½ cup finely chopped dried
   apricots
1 bag (10 ounces) large
   marshmallows
   (about 40)

½ cup (3 ounces) semisweet
   chocolate morsels
2 tablespoons milk
Vegetable cooking spray

Combine cereal, raisins, and apricots in large bowl; set aside.
Combine marshmallows, chocolate, and milk in 2-quart saucepan.
Place over low heat and cook, stirring, about 10 minutes or until
melted and smooth. Pour over cereal mixture; mix well. Coat
12×8×2-inch baking pan with cooking spray; spread mixture
evenly into pan. Press down firmly using fingers coated with
cooking spray. Cover and chill until firm. Cut into 1-inch squares.

Makes 8 dozen crispies

To microwave: Combine cereal, raisins, and apricots in large
bowl; set aside. Combine marshmallows, chocolate, and milk in
1½-quart microproof dish. Cook, uncovered, on HIGH 1 minute;
stir until smooth. Continue as directed above.

Tip: A great low-fat snack!

Favorite recipe from **USA Rice Federation**

Nutrients per Serving (1 crispie): Calories: 25, Calories from Fat: 14%,
Total Fat: <1 g, Protein: <1 g, Carbohydrate: 6 g, Cholesterol: 0 mg,
Sodium: 24 mg, Fiber: <1 g

Butterscotch Bars

¾ cup all-purpose flour
½ cup packed brown sugar
½ cup fat-free butterscotch
 ice cream topping
¼ cup cholesterol-free egg
 substitute

3 tablespoons margarine
 or butter, melted
1 teaspoon vanilla
¼ teaspoon salt
½ cup toasted chopped
 pecans (optional)

1. Preheat oven to 350°F. Lightly coat 8-inch square baking pan with nonstick cooking spray; set aside.

2. Combine all ingredients in medium bowl; stir until blended. Spread into prepared pan.

3. Bake 15 to 18 minutes or until firm to touch. Cool completely in pan. Cut into 16 bars.   *Makes 16 servings*

Tip: These sweet bars are the perfect packable treat. Wrap them individually in plastic wrap and they will be ready to grab for the lunch box or a spur-of-the-moment picnic in the park.

Nutrients per Serving: Calories: 95, Calories from Fat: 20%, Total Fat: 2 g, Saturated Fat: <1 g, Protein: 1 g, Carbohydrate: 18 g, Cholesterol: <1 mg, Sodium: 107 mg, Fiber: <1 g
Dietary Exchanges: 1 Starch, ½ Fat

Toasting nuts before using them in recipes intensifies their flavor, allowing you to use less of them. They also retain their crunch better than untoasted nuts.

Mixed Berry Tart with Ginger-Raspberry Glaze

1 refrigerated pie crust, at room temperature
¾ cup no-sugar-added seedless raspberry fruit spread
½ teaspoon grated fresh ginger or ¼ teaspoon ground ginger
2 cups fresh or frozen blueberries
2 cups fresh or frozen blackberries
1 peach, peeled and thinly sliced

1. Preheat oven 450°F. Coat 9-inch pie pan or tart pan with nonstick cooking spray. Carefully place pie crust on bottom of pan. Turn edges of pie crust inward to form ½-inch-thick edge. Press edges firmly against sides of pan. Using fork, pierce several times over entire bottom of pan to prevent crust from puffing up while baking. Bake 12 minutes or until golden brown. Cool completely on wire rack.

2. Heat fruit spread in small saucepan over high heat; stir until completely melted. Immediately remove from heat; stir in ginger and set aside to cool slightly.

3. Combine blueberries, blackberries and all but 2 tablespoons glaze; set aside.

4. Brush remaining 2 tablespoons glaze evenly over bottom of cooled crust. Decoratively arrange peach slices on top of crust and mound berries on top of peach slices. Refrigerate at least 2 hours. *Makes 8 servings*

Nutrients per Serving: Calories: 191, Calories from Fat: 33%, Total Fat: 7 g, Saturated Fat: 3 g, Protein: 1 g, Carbohydrate: 32 g, Cholesterol: 5 mg, Sodium: 172 mg, Fiber: 3 g
Dietary Exchanges: 1 Fruit, 1 Starch, 1½ Fat

Mixed Berry Tart with Ginger-Raspberry Glaze

Lemon Pound Cake with Strawberries

2 cups all-purpose flour
1 teaspoons baking powder
1 teaspoon baking soda
½ teaspoon salt
½ cup low-fat sour cream
½ cup fat-free (skim) milk
⅓ cup sugar
¼ cup vegetable oil
¼ cup cholesterol-free egg substitute
2 tablespoons lemon juice
1 teaspoon grated lemon peel
3 pints strawberries
Artificial sweetener (optional)

1. Preheat oven to 350°F. Coat 8×4-inch loaf pan with nonstick cooking spray. Combine flour, baking powder, baking soda and salt in large bowl.

2. Combine sour cream, milk, sugar, oil, egg substitute, lemon juice and lemon peel in medium bowl. Stir sour cream mixture into flour mixture until well combined; pour batter into prepared pan. Bake 45 to 50 minutes or until toothpick inserted in center comes out clean.

3. Let cake cool 20 minutes before removing from pan; cool completely. Meanwhile, slice strawberries. Sprinkle to taste with sweetener, if desired. Slice cake and serve with strawberries.

Makes 16 servings

Nutrients per Serving (1 slice): Calories: 180, Calories from Fat: 29%, Total Fat: 6 g, Saturated Fat: 1 g, Protein: 4 g, Carbohydrate: 28 g, Cholesterol: 4 mg, Sodium: 264 mg, Fiber: 2 g
Dietary Exchanges: 1 Fruit, 1 Starch, 1 Fat

Lemon Pound Cake with Strawberries

Chocolate Mint Meringues

3 egg whites
¾ teaspoon vanilla extract
¾ cup sugar

¼ cup HERSHEY'S Cocoa
Chocolate Mint Glaze
(recipe follows)

1. Heat oven to 300°F. Cover cookie sheet with parchment paper.

2. Beat egg whites and vanilla in large bowl on high speed of mixer until foamy. Beat in sugar, 1 tablespoon at a time, beating well after each addition until stiff peaks hold their shape, sugar is dissolved and mixture is glossy. Sift about half of cocoa over egg white mixture; gently fold in just until combined. Repeat with remaining cocoa.

3. Spoon mixture into pastry bag fitted with large star tip; pipe 2-inch-diameter stars onto prepared cookie sheet.

4. Bake 35 to 45 minutes or until dry. Cool slightly; peel paper from cookies. Cool completely on wire rack. Prepare Chocolate Mint Glaze.

5. Line tray or cookie sheet with wax paper. Dip half of each cookie into Chocolate Mint Glaze; place on prepared tray until set (refrigerate, if desired). Store, covered, in refrigerator.

Makes 3 dozen cookies

Chocolate Mint Glaze: Place ½ cup HERSHEY'S Semi-Sweet Chocolate Chips and 2 teaspoons shortening (do not use butter, margarine, spread or oil) in small microwave-safe bowl. Microwave at HIGH (100%) 1 minute or until chips are melted and mixture is smooth when stirred. Stir in 2 to 3 drops mint extract. Use immediately.

Nutrients per Serving: Calories: 31, Calories from Fat: 22%, Total Fat: 1 g, Saturated Fat: <1 g, Protein: 1 g, Carbohydrate: 6 g, Cholesterol: <1 mg, Sodium: 6 mg, Fiber: <1 g, Iron: <1 mg, Calcium: 2 mg, Vitamin A: 1 RE, Vitamin C: <1 mg, Sugar: 6 g
Dietary Exchanges: ½ Starch

Pear and Raspberry Strudel

½ cup no-sugar-added
    raspberry fruit spread
½ teaspoon ground
    cinnamon
4 ripe pears, peeled, cored
    and thinly sliced
1½ cups raspberries

10 sheets phyllo dough
    (about 18×14 inches)
Butter-flavored nonstick
    cooking spray
Low-fat, no-sugar-added
    ice cream (optional)

1. Preheat oven to 350°F. Combine fruit spread and cinnamon in small bowl; set aside. Combine pears and raspberries in large bowl.

2. Place 1 sheet phyllo dough on work surface. Keep remaining sheets covered with plastic wrap and damp kitchen towel. Lightly coat first phyllo sheet with nonstick cooking spray. Place second sheet on top of first; spray with cooking spray. Repeat process with remaining phyllo sheets.

3. Add fruit spread mixture to fruit. Spread fruit filling on phyllo to within 2 inches of edges. Starting at short sides, fold each over filling once. Beginning at long side, roll up jelly-roll fashion for roll about 14×5 inches. Place in jelly-roll pan. Lightly coat strudel with cooking spray. Cut diagonal slits about 1 inch apart and ½ inch deep along top of strudel.

4. Bake 30 minutes or until lightly browned. Cool 30 minutes. Slice diagonally into 12 pieces. Serve warm with ice cream, if desired. *Makes 12 servings*

Nutrients per Serving: Calories: 104, Calories from Fat: 9%, Total Fat: 1 g, Saturated Fat: <1 g, Protein: 1 g, Carbohydrate: 23 g, Cholesterol: 0 mg, Sodium: 88 mg, Fiber: 3 g
Dietary Exchanges: 1½ Fruit

Blueberry Bread Pudding with Caramel Sauce

Prep Time: 20 minutes   **Cook Time:** 1 hour

- 8 slices white bread, cubed
- 1 cup fresh or frozen blueberries
- 2 cups skim milk
- 1 cup EGG BEATERS® Healthy Real Egg Product
- ⅔ cup sugar
- 1 teaspoon vanilla extract
- ¼ teaspoon ground cinnamon
- Caramel Sauce (recipe follows)

Place bread cubes in bottom of lightly greased 8×8×2-inch baking pan. Sprinkle with blueberries; set aside.

In large bowl, combine milk, Egg Beaters®, sugar, vanilla and cinnamon; pour over bread mixture. Set pan in larger pan filled with 1-inch depth hot water. Bake at 350°F for 1 hour or until knife inserted in center comes out clean. Serve warm with Caramel Sauce.   *Makes 9 servings*

Caramel Sauce: In small saucepan, over low heat, heat ¼ cup skim milk and 14 vanilla caramels until caramels are melted, stirring frequently.

Nutrients per Serving: Calories: 196, Calories from Fat: 5%, Total Fat: 1 g, Saturated Fat: <1 g, Protein: 7 g, Carbohydrate: 40 g, Cholesterol: 1 mg, Sodium: 199 mg, Fiber: 1 g, Iron: 1 mg, Calcium: 113 mg, Vitamin A: 66 RE, Vitamin C: 3 mg, Sugar: 24 g
Dietary Exchanges: ½ Fruit, 2 Starch, ½ Fat

Blueberry Bread Pudding with
Caramel Sauce

Acknowledgments

The publisher would like to thank the companies and organizations listed below for the use of their recipes and photographs in this publication.

Butterball® Turkey Company

Campbell Soup Company

Colorado Potato Administrative Committee

Del Monte Corporation

Dole Food Company, Inc.

Egg Beaters®

Fleischmann's® Original Spread

Guiltless Gourmet®

Hershey Foods Corporation

Kellogg Company

The Kingsford Products Company

Lipton®

National Honey Board

National Pork Producers Council

New York Apple Association, Inc.

The Procter & Gamble Company

Sunkist Growers

Uncle Ben's Inc.

USA Rice Federation

Index